GAINER'S GOURMET

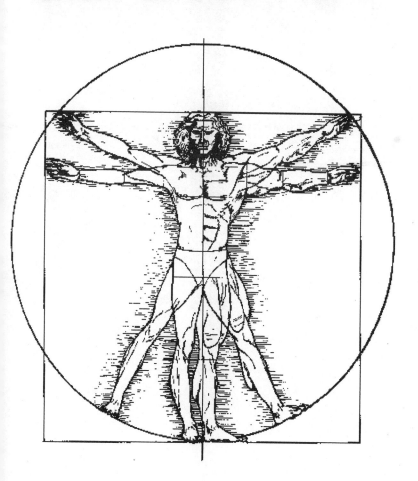

GAINER'S GOURMET
RECIPES FOR MASS

by
Faith Walker

Published by Lion Attitude

Published by:
Lion Attitude
P.O.Box 2055
Venice, CA 90294 USA

Library of Congress catalogue card number:
92-090495

ISBN 0-9633879-0-1

Cover & Interior Illustrations, Photography,
Design and Production:
Leon

Editor: Hope Elizabeth Bauch

We would like to thank all of those who have offered their consistant positive support and tastebuds—Mom and Dad, Steve and Becky Holman, Jerry Robinson and Nadine Sondej, Randall Strossen, Stuart McRobert, and last but not least John Balik.

CONTENTS

BEEF ETC

EGGS

FISH

PASTA

POTATOES

POULTRY

MISC. SNACKS AND STUFF

"We may live without poetry, music and art,
We may live without conscience, and live
without heart;
We may live without friends; we may live
without books;
But civilized man cannot live without cooks."

E.R. Bulwer-Lytton, 1860

INTRODUCTION: EATING BIG

Dietary advice and information have become incredibly general in our present time. Although certain dietary guidelines have been established and deemed healthy and appropriate by a few, this does not mean they should be accepted by all. This book goes against the general theories and the way they tend to be applied to all people regardless of their metabolism or lifestyle.

Diet is a very personal thing. People who are aspiring to gain weight, not maintain it, and especially those individuals who bodybuild, do not fit into the neat package of John Q. Public. Why would someone who wants to be above average physically subscribe to an average diet?

Hardgainers are different. I know, I am one. We have different metabolisms from most people, and we participate in a sport which most average people call different (many call it more than that, but we'll leave it there).

This is a book written for you as a hardgainer specifically, whether you want to be hugely muscular or just comfortably out of the "skinny" catagory. At last, no-nonsense, common sense nutrition, written for hardgainers by a hardgainer. Welcome to the world of food. It's going to make a lot more impact on your journey to a better body than the latest supplement fad.

I believe strongly that luck is when preparation meets opportunity. Good luck to all!

Faith Walker 1992

"If you want to look young and thin, hang around old fat people."

Jim Eason

SERVINGS DEFINED

You will notice that with each recipe comes an approximate serving count listing the calories, protein, carbohydrate and fat breakdown (rounded to the nearest gram) for each serving. I figured those out as a courtesy to people who are tabulating those for their own use in structuring their diet. It is somewhat ironic, though, listing them at all, simply because most people who are actually counting out specific grams wouldn't touch my recipes with a ten foot pole because of the high fat content. Most hardgainers or ectomorphs needn't bother themselves with caloric breakdowns. Some of you, though, may wish to gather an approximate idea of calories and categories, to keep a general plan of protein, carbohydrates and fat intake.

One definite reason why my breakdowns look bigger then most (in all categories) is that when I say three servings, for example, I mean three hearty platefuls of food. If you've been reading labels, then you probably have become accustomed to the misleading practice of listing many servings. A big can of tuna, for example, lists 6.3 servings. This might suffice for small children, but for two people who exercise regularly, tend to be thin, and have hearty appetites, one can of 12 1/2 oz tuna would be just enough. By making the servings higher, the fat content looks much lower. What it boils down to is that it is what you eat that counts, not what you read. Although the breakdowns may look excessive, they are realistic (like what you see in the mirror).

"I prefer Hostess fruit pies to pop-up toaster tarts because they don't require so much cooking."

Carrie Snow

KITCHEN HELP

Cooking really isn't a hard thing to do, really. Many people have a sort of phobia about the kitchen. I think it's similar to being an artist in the way that, just by producing something, you are [in a way] opening yourself up to the possible negative reviews of those exposed to your creation. Cooking, whether you find it enjoyable or not, is something that pretty much has to be done (unless you are lucky enough to marry someone like me). If you are going to put on muscle you have absolutely no alternative but to exercise, and the same goes for eating. It can at times be an annoying interruption to our schedules, but being hungry is not, generally speaking, a desirable state of mind.

There are many things you can do to make this seemingly endless task less time consuming. The first is having a decently stocked kitchen. This doesn't mean a financial outlay the size of your gym membership, but a small investment. If you take some of the money you may use on supplements and invest it in utensils, you will undoubtedly be better off. I don't have an extraordinarily well-stocked kitchen; in fact, there really aren't that many things that are indispensable. To this day I still haven't gotten around to buying a cookie sheet. I just use my glass oblong pan. Here goes:

1 Good Chopping Knife
1 Good Slicing Knife
Garlic Crusher
Shredder or Salad Shooter
Basic Food Processor
Large Cast Iron Skillet
Saucepan
Soup Pot

Oblong Glass Pan
Glass Loaf Pan
Casserole Dish with Lid

Along with these items there are some herbs and seasoning mixes that can take the guesswork out of many dishes and really zip up your basic fare.

Garlic Powder
Chili Powder
Dried Parsley
Italian Seasoning
Fish Seasoning
Poultry Seasoning
Vegetable Seasoning
Pepper
Cumin
Cayenne Pepper
Red Wine Vinegar
White Wine Vinegar
Worchestershire Sauce

Other things are nice to have: Thyme, Basil, Oregano, etc., but with the basics above you can always get by. Making scrambled eggs? Throw a little Vegetable Seasoning in there. Basic spaghetti? Add some Italian Seasoning. Chili? A little extra Chili Powder. All of a sudden people will think you are a much better cook. Those pre-made seasonings are great, someone else did all the footwork on figuring out which blends and amounts work best, and most of them did a terrific job.

When shopping at the grocery store you'll find that if you stock up on certain basics there will always be something you can whip up for a good healthy meal. Try these for starters:

Cans of Tuna
Milk, Bread, Eggs, Cheese and Butter
Yogurt
Vegetarian Refried Beans

Cans of chili
Rice, regular and quick-cooking
Pasta and Pasta Sauce
Onions and Potatoes
Bananas

With these few ingredients (not even counting any meat) there are many meals you can make quickly and simply, and it's much healthier usually than eating out.

I have taken the liberty of suggesting brand names throughout the cookbook. It has been through endless label-reading and taste-testing that I have been led to those particular brands, and hopefully you can benefit from my time spent combing the grocery aisles. It should be added that fresh anything is best. The less processed the food you are eating is, the more nutrition you will derive from it. In the quest for time efficiency, though, there are reasonable substitutions for home-made, and I have used them when possible to make the recipes less demanding.

A kitchen is a homey, comfortable place. Ever notice at parties how everyone generally hangs out in the kitchen? For most people eating is fun, and for us (hardgainers) eating is especially fun because we can smother our foodstuffs with all kinds of decadent and delicious ingredients, as long as we are working out like demons anyway! I hope this book will help the bond between you and your kitchen grow stronger; and, if you were intimidated before you should be more confident. If you are already a good cook then I hope you get a few ideas of your own from my experiments. Any way you look at it, eating is generally a happy time; and if these tips have helped make the daily meal more enjoyable then I'll have accomplished at least one of the goals I had with writing this book.

"Common sense is in spite of, not the result of, education."

Victor Hugo

EAT IT RAW

For years people have belittled me for spending extra money (and time) to purchase organic and quality items at specialty and health food stores. The argument against making this extra effort is that there is no proof whatsoever that the foods I buy are organic, since there is little or no regulatory control. I say buy it and taste it, whatever the item may be—an organic apple, for example. It may not be as big or as beautiful as the typical grocery store variety, but, given the difference in taste and freshness, you will become accustomed to the superior quality. Quality and organically-grown foods can dramatically improve the success rate of your cooking, and fresher nuts, vegetables and meats are much higher in nutrients.

There is another important reason to buy organic: You show your support for natural farming, and you give the more industrial-oriented farming and meat-raising companies a nudge in the pocketbook to swing away from the pesticides and chemicals they presently use. If you are opposed to steroid and hormone use in bodybuilding, then it doesn't make sense to ingest them in the meat you're buying at the supermarket. Natural foods are more expensive, but the old axiom holds true: You get what you pay for.

Fresh, raw and/or organic is definitely best. This is true of both dairy products and produce. Let's tackle the dairy products first. For most hardgainers, dairy foods are a caloric as well as nutritional necessity. Nearly all commercial dairy products are pasteurized and homogenized, which means they went through processes in which they were heated to very high temperatures in order to kill bacteria. These processes, however, also kill nearly all of the beneficial properties and reduce the product's overall nutrient content so when it comes to milk, cheese and butter, Raw is King.

Unfortunately , raw products aren't available everywhere, and where you can get them they're usually more expensive than the processed variety. Although they're strictly regulated (more so than standard commercial fare), they still carry the taboo factor for most uninformed shoppers. The powers that be who created this scare are the same folks who told us that eggs were killing us (and who recently admitted that they're not nearly as bad as was originally believed).

There are many things you can do to increase the nutritional value of your dairy consumption even if raw products are not within your financial reach or readily available. When purchasing cheese, for example, buy aged cheese. Aged cheeses are generally made with raw cultured milk. Buy real butter instead of margarine. Margarine contains hydrogenated oils, stabilizers, colorings, preservatives and other assorted chemicals. There are, however, higher quality margarines available at health food stores.

Another few words should be said about dairy products and milk in particular. A small percentage of adults lack the ability to digest milk and/or various dairy products comfortably. Though raw milk and raw dairy products are superior in quality, they still should be ingested with caution. Stuart McRobert suggested simplifying your milk consumption by trying to take care in what your milk is combined with, as the combination itself may irritate a more sensitive digestive system. Freddie Lindblad, who was nutritionally educated by Rheo Blair, taught us early on that milk in itself is a meal and an invaluable bodybuilding food. If you are suspicious about your ability to digest milk, try to listen to your system and proceed with caution in the Pro-Drink Chapter.

Randall Strossen, who is a firm believer in milk as

a "premier bodybuilding food", made some good suggestions also. Apparently many lactose-intolerant people can drink milk if they gradually introduce themselves to it. Also, many who cannot drink ordinary milk can drink acidophilus milk or use lact-aid, available in most health-food stores. You might want to give these alternatives a go before giving up entirely.

As far as sweeteners go, raw is king once again. Try using raw honey, maple syrup, apple juice concentrate or even molasses instead of sugar. These sweeteners don't contain any additives or undergo the bleaching that white sugar is subjected to before it's considered fit for consumption.

Produce is incredibly good for you when you eat it raw. It goes without saying that organic produce is best. If it is even a fraction healthier with even slightly less chemicals, then it's probably going to look worse but taste better. An organic apple may not be as presentable as a perfect-looking, waxed one, but where it's going (in your stomach) nobody's going to see it! I'd rather have a healthy-looking body in a bikini than a healthy-looking apple in my cooler.

Many things happen to our fruits and vegetables before they get to the local supermarket. These foods are much more nutritious when allowed to ripen on the plant. You could say that they develop to their full potential that way. Because of lengthy transit times to the market many items are picked green and then stored for weeks. Some types of produce, such as bananas and tomatoes, are even gassed to continue the ripening process.

It is for this reason that, occasionally, frozen items can actually be more nutritious. Vegetables are indispensable in your diet so, if the pickings are slim, frozen is the way to go. I've found that frozen organic vegetables are really tasty and sweet. With the combined pluses of natural soil and extended ripening on the plant you can't go wrong.

Here are a few things you can do to maintain the content of your produce purchases:

☞ **Avoid prolonged soaking or precutting of fruits and vegies; this causes them to lose some of their nutrients.**

☞ **Cook vegies only until they are tender but still crisp. Overcooking breaks down the vegies and leachs many nutrients from them.**

☞ **Try not to peel fruits and vegies unless it's absolutely necessary. It's kind of a double-edged sword. On one hand, many of the food's beneficial nutrients are contained in the peel or skin. On the other hand, the outer skin is often exposed to pesticides, waxes and gasses.**

Raw foods can offer many advantages over cooked or processed foods. The fibers are in an unprocessed natural state, something your body can use immediately. Think about the chemicals and highly processed products we expect our bodies to derive nutritional value from. Isn't it possible that we might not be able to process some of these substances that we can't even pronounce? The body may excrete them from our pores or spend precious energy trying vainly to digest them.

So give it some thought. Many people claim that vegetarianism is the answer, but I disagree. Presently, with the amounts of chemicals used to grow commercial produce, your vegetarian diet may not be as healthy as you might think. More planning and more thought as to whose hands your hard-earned cash ends up in can make a tremendous difference in your diet. Both the quality and quantity of the food you buy will be affected. Where you spend your money determines the fate of virtually every product on the market. If the commercial companies start feeling everyone's purchasing power swaying to a different tune, you can bet your next paycheck they'll be scrambling to fill that need.

SOME OPINIONATED WORDS ABOUT FAT...

Since this book is about eating and diet, and since you are buying this book on the assumption that these recipes are good (and good for you), I feel obligated to you as a reader and as a friend to share my thoughts and what I've learned about diet in regard to fat consumption. Many people will vehemently disagree, and that's good, because out of disagreement and the search for knowledge comes advancement. It is important to state right off the bat that a high fat diet is obviously not going to work for everyone. To a person with a very slow metabolism or a tendency towards high cholesterol this cookbook is not for you! Of course an occasional, high calorie or high fat meal is not that big a deal for even the slowest metabolism, but on the whole those people do have diets far from the one I am suggesting.

While it is a fact that I continue to endorse a high-fat diet (devoid of sugars, white flour and processed foods as much as possible) I never have and never will be one to tell you that I prefer an overweight physique to lean, defined muscle. I'm talking about eating fat, not wearing it. Fat is energy; that is a very important thing to keep in mind. Fat is necessary for your body to function at an optimum level, especially while bodybuilding. Your energy level is going to determine (along with other factors, of course) the success of your workouts. If you happen to have a high metabolism, then I'm sure you've encountered the problem of running out of steam in the gym. With our busy lifestyles today sometimes it comes down to eating *or* going to the gym. What I'm suggesting here is that going to the gym on an empty tank, so to speak, is a big waste of time. Without the proper fuel you are just cannibalizing whatever muscle you may have managed to build, and thus you are beginning the one step forward, two steps back routine. Eating right and eating for strength can make a tremendous difference in the progress of your weightlifting. Bodybuilding is a process of progressive resistance, progressive meaning increments of more weight and more weight over the course of time. In order to lift that additional weight your body will have to build more muscle. The importance of the proper fuel can determine the ability of your body to keep up with that progression of work. The whole concept of your getting a bigger, more muscular physique is really that simple. You need to lift heavier weights, while at the same time providing your body the rest and food intake necessary to recuperate and keep up with the work load. Remember I said simple, not easy.

In this book of recipes I have included a breakdown of calories, protein, carbs and fat. I feel quite strongly that hardgainers should not pay too much attention to these. Let the most powerful bodybuilding tool available be your guide: the mirror. The mirror (and maybe your mate) will clearly let you know if your fat and food consumption is getting out of hand. It is important that you don't expect yourself to remain completely ripped at all times while gaining massive inches of miraculous muscle. That's about what it would be, miraculous. Living here in Venice and working at Ironman has given me the opportunity to see many bodybuilders, natural and otherwise, in both contest and off-season condition. Let me tell you that in the off season they do not look like the ripped corded specimens of beef that you see in the magazine. These people are photographed in top condition. That's something that is achieved by a strict exercise and food diet. Nine out of ten bodybuilders do look beautiful and impressive in any season, but there are times when more fat is allowed, allowing them the energy and strength needed to press the heavy poundages to ensure more growth in the right places. Natural bodybuilders will want to do the same. If the name of the game is putting on some size, allow a little extra weight on your physique. A very respected natural lifter put it to me this way: You can gain ten pounds, take off five and you still keep the other five in pure muscle. This is a slow and steady process, generally taking years to accumulate enough until you look in that handy mirror up and down, front and back and say, yeah, this is more like it.

Fats are digested more slowly then other foods. Meat, as you know, stays with you a lot longer than even the biggest helping of vegetables. Meat is important to a thin person trying to put on weight. Since it is harder to digest, it may be a good idea to consume meat in smaller amounts if necessary, and be sure to keep your diet loaded with fresh vegetables and fruits at the same time. Generally your body will crave foods that it needs (no, I don't mean sweets). While one week you may find yourself eating meat three or four times, it may be a couple of weeks before you need it, or crave it, again. The same can be said for dairy products, which are high in calories and fat. Dairy products can be a great help to your diet and workouts; but, by the same token, if your body has hit its tolerance level and they just don't sound appetizing to you, then listen to yourself. YOU know how you feel. Everyone else only knows how you feel based on what you convey, or tell them, about how you feel. These two may be very different depending on how accurate your description, and also how much personal information you are willing to tell someone.

When choosing foods many people make the mistake of letting the fat content rule the decision to eat it or not. I seriously doubt if you would buy a car without looking at the engine or a house without looking at the interior. Why then is everyone so willing to eat a food without regard to its content or quality of ingredients but only its label? Most foods and ingredients didn't come with this kind of breakdown many years ago, so why has it become so important in our diet today? Because "They" told you a high fat diet was bad for you, right? Phooey. "They" don't know your exercise schedule, or your energy level, or your digestive system; you do. One habit to break immediately, if you are going to put some weight on your bones, is assuming that any food is bad for you just because the almighty "They" said so. "They" probably sell you a lot of magarine, egg subsitutes, lowfat milk, lowfat this and lowfat that. Most of this stuff is over-processed and loaded with ingredients and chemicals that take the place of the so-called evil fat. Hardly a healthful trade-off, but a big financial gain for "They".

Remember, fat is energy, fat is strength, and in the right amounts (the mirror helpfully will guide you) fat is good for you.

———————————

"Whenever I'm caught between two evils,
I take the one I've never tried"

Mae West

"A man seldom thinks with more earnestness of anything than he does of his dinner."

Samuel Johnson, 1786

BRAIN FOOD / BODY FOOD

Vince Gironda used to tell us when we were training at his gym, "Look out there," (pointing to the gym area), "that's iron. That's not what makes a body-builder. It's what's in here, (pointing above each ear), that's what builds a body! That out there is just iron, that's not going to make you stronger, this is what you need to develop—between your ears!" Many things are going to contribute to your success, and they are all going to depend on how you use your noggin.

Your frame of mind is going to affect, dramatically, the effectiveness of your diet and food intake. Jack LaLanne in his Set-O-Matic book of exercises put it this way: "Keep cheerful and happy when you are eating, and keep reminding yourself that all the good foods that you are eating are building you a vibrant, healthy body." When you are upset, stressed or overtrained your digestion clearly will be affected. Most people react in one extreme or another when faced with trauma or depression, either gorging themselves or almost completely abstaining from food—equally unhealthy, unfortunately.

To be healthy and develop a strong healthy body, think of "feeding" yourself some positive thoughts. Try keeping an eye on your brain's diet! What kind of food intake are you giving it as you talk to yourself?

If you are a natural bodybuilder, chances are that you have a tendency to overtrain and thus impede your progress. Rest is not just important, it's CRUCIAL. The quality of your rest can determine the success of your next workout. If your muscles are still tired, they are going to feel tired, and chances are you might get down on yourself for a wimpy workout, thus feeding your brain some real garbage.

The food you eat when taking a rest day or week is

a stepping stone to your bodybuilding progress. First, the brain food: Positive, happy reassuring food, easy to digest. Try confirming to yourself how great this rest i. how you are really going to kick-butt when you get back to the gym, how important this time off really is, and how you have the opportunity to spend time with friends and family, or pursue another hobby or sport. There is, after all, life outside the gym. Second, your body's food. It is very possible, especially if you are ta ing a week off (which I highly recommend every coup of months) that you are going to have to adjust your eating habits. It's important to keep in mind that keep ing up the same intake amounts while reducing your exercise routine is a sure-fire way to ensure added weight in the wrong places. This may lead you to thin you shouldn't have taken the break. Wrong. You should have used your most powerful tool, your brain better, and realized, a cutback on your workout should accompany a reduction in food intake.

It is especially important when you are going outside of your established dietary guidelines, or splurgin in other words, that you thoroughly enjoy every bite. Compounding the splurge with a lot of negative thoughts will double the impact of the digression, mal ing what probably shouldn't be a big deal into one.

It's important that you be realistic with your menta goals and thoughts. After all, it is a fact that you can "think" all you want; and that's not going to take the place of applying your mental discipline in the gym. We each have our own genetics to deal with, that's a given. As hardgainers we have a lot of physical work do. How far we go in changing our bodies is limited t not only how determined we are but also to the inten: ty and consistency that we exercise (no pun intended) that determination.

"A hungry man is an angry man."

James Howard, 1659

"All of us, when well, give good
advice to the sick."

Terence: Andria, II, c. 160 B.C.

RECOMMENDED READING

Nutrition:

Dr. Wright's Guide To Healing with Nutrition/Jonathan
V. Wright, M.D.
Human Fuel Handbook/Health for Life
Lean for Life/Clarence Bass
Nutrition Almanac
Zane Nutrition/Frank and Christine Zane

Cookbooks:

The Enchanted Broccoli Forest/Molly Katzen
Zane Nutrition/Frank and Christine Zane

Workout & Routine Info:

Brawn/Stuart McRobert
Home Gym Handbook/Steve Holman
Super Squats/Randall Strossen

"Men of great abilities are generally of a
large and vigorous animal nature."

Henry Taylor: The Statesman, 1836

BEEF

"Better to pay the butcher than
the doctor."

German proverb

LIVER WITH RICE

1 Beef Liver
1 Onion, chopped
3 Tb Butter
1 Cup Rice
28 oz can Tomatoes

▲ Cook Rice
▲ Brown Onions in Butter, remove from pan
▲ Cook chopped Liver (bite-sized pieces) in Butter until done
▲ Layer the ingredients in a casserole dish—first the Onions, then the Liver, then the Rice and then top it all off with the Tomatoes
▲ Bake in 350 degree oven for about 20 minutes

4 Servings

Calories: 392
Protein: 22
Carb: 43
Fat: 14

Liver is liver, and for me this is as good as it gets.

LIVER AND ONIONS

4 Slices Bacon
1 Onion, chopped
1 Beef Liver (about 8oz)

▲ Cook Bacon, remove from pan
▲ Saute Onion until brown, remove from pan
▲ Cook Liver until desired consistency
▲ Cut Liver in half, top each piece with Onions and Bacon strips

2 Servings

Calories: 349
Protein: 35
Carbs: 15
Fat: 25

MEATLOAF

2 lbs Ground Beef
2 Eggs
1 Chopped Onion
2 Garlic cloves, crushed
1/2 Cup Oats
2 Tb Ketchup
1 tsp Worchester
1 tsp Cumin Powder

- Put all ingredients in a large bowl and mix together (hands do the best job)
- Pat into glass loaf pan
- Bake at 350 degrees 1 hour 15 min

4 Servings

Calories: 435
Protein: 32
Carbs: 13
Fat: 28

Excellent for dinner the first night and sandwiches the next day.

MEXICAN MEATLOAF

1 lb Ground Beef
1 Onion, chopped
1 Bell Pepper, chopped
1 Cup Peas
1 Egg
1 Cup Bread Crumbs (3 slices of stale bread in a food processor)
1 tsp Chili Powder
1/2 tsp Salt
1 14 1/2 oz can S&W Mexican Style Stewed Tomatoes

▲ Mix everything but Tomatoes together and pat into a casserole dish
▲ Pour Tomatoes over the top
▲ Bake at 375 degrees for 1 hour

5 Servings

Calories: 292
Protein: 26
Carbs: 16
Fat: 14

This is a great change from ordinary meatloaf and makes ideal leftovers.

BEEFY BURRITOS

1 lb Ground Beef
1 Onion, chopped
1 packet Taco Seasoning
1/4 Cup Sour Cream (approx)
1 Cup Shredded Jack Cheese
5 Large Flour Tortillas

▲ Brown Beef and Onions, drain
▲ Add Taco Seasoning, cook according to directions
▲ Warm Tortilla on both sides in a skillet
▲ Put a large spoonful of Beef down the middle, sprinkle
   with Cheese, add approx 1 Tb Sour Cream
▲ Fold ends up to Beef, fold one long side over and roll up
▲ Keep in warm oven until all are done

Per Burrito

Calories: 496
Protein: 36
Carbs: 31
Fat: 25

Great weekend dinner with plenty of Cerveza, and don't forget the chips and salsa!

TORTILLA PIE

1 lb Ground Beef
1 Onion, chopped
2 Tb Chili Powder
2 Tb Butter
5 Whole Wheat Tortillas
1 4 oz can Diced Green Chilis
1 1/2 Cups Shredded Monterey Jack Cheese
1 10 3/4 oz can of Cream of Mushroom soup
1/2 Cup Salsa (I like Pace Picante Sauce)

▲ Brown Beef and Onions in skillet
▲ Drain off fat, remove to a bowl and stir in Chili Powder
▲ Melt Butter in clean skillet
▲ Heat Tortillas on both sides, one at a time
▲ Layer Tortilla, Chilis, Beef then Cheese until out of
  ingredients (a round casserole dish works best)
▲ Pour soup over top, then salsa on top of that
▲ Bake at 325 degrees for 30 minutes

6 Servings

Calories: 613
Protein: 40
Carbs: 27
Fat: 36

This is a very rich and very tasty dish, kind of like a
Mexican Stroganoff!

BEEF LASAGNA

28 oz can Peeled Tomatoes (I like Progresso Italian style)
1/4 lb Sliced Mushrooms (about 3 Cups)
1/4 Cup Red Wine
1 Tb Italian Seasoning
1 can Black Olives, sliced
1 lb Ground Beef
1 Onion, chopped
2 Garlic cloves, crushed
15 oz container Ricotta Cheese
10 oz frozen Spinach, thawed and drained
16 oz package Lasagne noodles
16 oz Mozzarella, in thin slices
3 Tb grated Parmesan Cheese

▲ Rough chop the Tomatoes, add the first four ingredients together (You can do this ahead of time to let the flavors blend)
▲ Saute the Beef, Onion and Garlic, drain
▲ Mix the Ricotta and Spinach together in a bowl
▲ Cook the Noodles in a very large pot of water (or they'll all stick together), Drain, then rinse with cold water and drain again
▲ Starting with the Sauce, layer Noodles, Spinach mix, Beef and finally Mozzarella, until reaching the top of a glass oblong pan
▲ Top with the Parmesan Cheese
▲ Bake at 350 degrees for approx 45 minutes

8 Servings

Calories: 673
Protein: 45
Carbs: 55
Fat: 30

HAMBURGER GRUEL AND BROWN RICE

1 lb Ground Beef
1 Onion, chopped
2 Garlic cloves, crushed
1 10 3/4 can of Cream of Mushroom soup
1 can Milk (use soup can)
2 cups cooked Brown Rice

▲ Put the Rice on first; by the time it's done the gravy will be ready
▲ Brown Beef with Onion and Garlic, drain
▲ Add soup, slowly stir in Milk
▲ Simmer about 10 minutes
▲ Pour over Rice and Serve

4 Servings

Calories: 524
Protein: 38
Carbs: 38
Fat: 23

Quick and easy. Not for company, but great for an every day meal of which there are oh so many.

BEEF AND POTATOES

1 lb Ground Beef
1 Onion, sliced
Salt, Pepper, Garlic powder and Oregano
1 large Bell Pepper, sliced
3 small Potatoes, sliced (no need to peel)
1 14 1/2 oz can Tomatoes (S&W recipe-ready are great)

▲ Brown Beef and Onions, drain
▲ Sprinkle generously with seasonings and stir well
▲ Layer Beef, Potatoes and Bell Peppers in a casserole dish, ending with Beef
▲ Top with can of Tomatoes
▲ Bake at 350 degrees for 1 hour

4 Very Hearty Servings

Calories: 445
Protein: 35
Carbs: 34
Fat: 20

Good with steamed broccoli, or corn on the cob. Very good for the microwave the next day (the spices set in and it's even better). This one is a pain in the neck if you don't have a salad shooter to do the slicing!

SLOPPY SPUDS

1 lb Ground Beef
1 Onion, chopped
2 Garlic cloves, crushed
1 4 oz can Tomato Paste
1 cup Water
1 4 oz can sliced Black Olives
1 1/2 tsp Cumin
4 Potatoes
1 Cup Cheddar Cheese, grated

▲ Bake the potatoes in a 375 degree oven for approx one hour or until they give when you squeeze them
▲ Brown the Beef, Onions and Garlic, drain
▲ Add the Tomato Paste, Water, Cumin, Olives and stir, keeping the burner on simmer.
▲ Continue to simmer for about 20 minutes
▲ Beat the Potatoes up by banging them against a hard surface, slice them down the middle once and across several times
▲ Spoon the Tomato Mixture over the Potatoes and top with Cheddar Cheese

4 Servings

Calories: 635
Protein: 41
Carbs: 59
Fat: 26

Unique and delicous, pretty easy too!

BARBELL BEANS

2 lbs Ground Beef
2 Tb Oil
1 Large Onion, chopped
1 Bell Pepper, chopped
2 Garlic cloves, minced
2 Tb Chili Powder
1 tsp Cayenne Pepper
1 tsp Ground Cumin
28 oz can Tomatoes, chopped
1/2 can Black Olives, chopped
1 15 1/4 oz can Kidney Beans, drained
1 15 1/4 oz can Pinto Beans, drained
Sour Cream

▲ Brown the Beef, drain and set aside
▲ Saute the Onion, Bell Pepper and Garlic in Oil until limp
▲ Put the Beef and Vegies in a large pot and add the rest
▲ Cover and cook for about 30 minutes
▲ Top each serving with Sour Cream

8 Large Servings

Calories: 533
Protein: 43
Carbs: 33
Fat: 28

Oh man, this Chili and a beer is worth a lot of working out.

CHILI PORK STIR FRY

4 Tb Oil
1 Tb Red Wine Vinegar
1 Tb Chili Powder
1/4 Tsp Cumin
1 Onion, sliced
2 Garlic cloves, crushed
1 Red Bell Pepper, thinly sliced
4 Pork Chops, cut from bone

suggestion
1 Can French Onion Soup
Brown Rice (1/2 of soup amount)

▲ Stir Rice into hot soup, cover, and cook approx 1 hr
▲ Heat Oil, Vinegar, Chili Powder and Cumin in large skillet
▲ Add Onions and Garlic, saute until Onion is wilted slightly
▲ Add Bell Pepper and saute for about 30 more seconds
▲ Push Vegies aside and add Pork. Cook for approx 4 minutes, flip, and cook until done. Try not to overcook, cut pieces in half to check for pinkness
▲ Top with Vegies and sauce, serve with Rice

2 Large Servings (breakdown doesn't include Rice)

Calories: 889
Protein: 66
Carbs: 13
Fat: 63

Kind of spicy and very, very good. The rice goes well with this.

"Reminds me of my safari in Africa. Somebody forgot the corkscrew and for several days we had to live on nothing but food and water."

W.C. Fields

"You can't unscramble scrambled eggs."

American proverb

EGGS

"Those who do not find time for exercise
will have to find time for illness."

The Earl of Derby, 1873

EGGS AND SQUASH

2 Whole Eggs
3 Egg Whites
2 Tb Butter
3 Chopped Green Onions
1 Zucchini, sliced
1 Yellow Crookneck Squash, sliced
1/4 tsp Vegetable Seasoning
1 Tb Grated Parmesan Cheese

▲ Beat Eggs and Egg Whites
▲ Saute Vegies in Butter and Seasoning until slightly cooked
▲ Lower heat slightly
▲ Pour Eggs over Vegies, cover and cook until set
▲ Sprinkle Parmesan over the top
▲ Fold one side over the other (This is where things might not go so smoothly, don't worry about it, it'll taste the same.)

2 Servings

Calories: 257
Protein: 14
Carbs: 9
Fat: 19

You can cut the fat to 7 grams by eliminating the butter, but if you are looking for calories you will sacrifice those also, bringing the calorie count down to 149.

SPINACH SCRAMBLE

1 lb Ground Beef
1 Onion, sliced
2 Garlic cloves, crushed
5 Eggs
1/4 Cup Milk
10 oz frozen Spinach, thawed and drained
1/2 Cup shredded Cheddar
1/2 Avocado, sliced

▲ Beat Eggs and Milk together
▲ Brown and drain Beef, Onion and Garlic
▲ Pour in Egg mixture, let it cook for a minute or so
▲ Add Spinach and stir in
▲ Continue cooking, stirring occasionally until done
▲ Sprinkle Cheese on top, cover or stir in to melt it
▲ Serve with sliced Avocado

4 Servings

Calories: 537
Protein: 47
Carbs: 11
Fat: 34

The breakdown includes the avocado which is very high in fat but also very nutritious and complementary to this dish.

SCRAMBLED EGGS WITH CREAM CHEESE AND BACOS

6 Eggs, beaten
4 oz Cream Cheese, cut into small cubes
1 Tb Bacos or crumbled Bacon

▲ Pour Eggs into heated non-stick or oiled skillet
▲ Cook until almost done
▲ Add Cream Cheese and Bacos, stir together well
▲ Serve when Eggs are done and the Cream Cheese begins
to melt

2 Servings

Calories: 456
Protein: 24
Carbs: 5
Fat: 75

Very rich and delicious, sticks to your ribs for a long time.
When buying bacon bits be sure to read the labels, you
could accidentaly end up with some scary stuff if you don't.

BREAKFAST BURRITOS

1 Cooked Potato
1/2 Onion, sliced
4 Eggs, beaten
1 Tb Butter
1/2 Cup Shredded Cheddar Cheese
4 Flour Tortillas
Salsa to taste

▲ Cut Potato into small cubes
▲ Melt Butter in skillet
▲ Saute Onions
▲ Add Eggs and scramble
▲ Fill warmed Tortillas with Eggs and Onions, Potatoes, Cheese and Salsa and roll into burritos
▲ Keep in a warmed oven until they are all ready

Per Burrito (Makes 4)

Calories: 310
Protein: 14
Carbs: 30
Fat: 15

This is an easy recipe to modify. You easily can omit the yolks, use no cheese and more salsa, etc.

SPANISH SCRAMBLE

5 Eggs
1/4 Cup Milk
4 Corn Tortillas, cut in small squares
2 Tb Butter
5 Green Onions, chopped
1/2 Cup Cheddar Cheese, grated
Salsa, optional

▲ Beat Eggs and Milk together until well blended
▲ Saute Corn Tortilla squares in Butter until semi-crispy
▲ Add Eggs, stir and cook until almost done
▲ Add Green Onions and Cheese, cook until desired consistency
▲ Top with Salsa if preferred

2 Hearty Servings

Calories: 567
Protein: 27
Carbs: 30
Fat: 38

Courtesy of Hope.

CRUNCHY EGG SALAD SANDWICHE

5 Hard Boiled Eggs
1 Dill Pickle, chopped
1 Stalk Celery, chopped
2 Tb minced Red Onion (about 1/4 onion)
2 Tb Mayo
1 Tb White Wine Vinegar
Salt and Pepper
6 Slices Wheat Bread, lightly buttered

▲ Mash first six ingredients together thoroughly
▲ Salt and Pepper to taste
▲ Divide filling into 3 sandwiches

Per Sandwich

Calories: 360
Protein: 15
Carbs: 25
Fat: 23

Much better (in my opinion) then regular egg salad

DEVILED EGGS

6 Hard Boiled Eggs
1 Tb Mayo
White Wine Vinegar
Salt
Pepper
Paprika

▲ Cut eggs in half lengthwise
▲ Pop yolks out into a bowl
▲ Add Mayo, about 4 splashes of Wine Vinegar, and Salt &
  Pepper
▲ Mix thoroughly, spoon mixture into whites
▲ Sprinkle with Paprika

2 (3 Egg) Servings

Calories: 266
Protein: 19
Carbs: 4
Fat: 19

There is good fat and bad fat. Example: Bad fat—
Chocolate chip cookies. Good fat— Eggs. Don't let the
fat content on this one scare you away. Eggs are a good
Hardgainer food.

"In Mexico we have a word for sushi: bait."

Jose Simon

FISH

"He that takes medicine and neglects to diet wastes the skills of his doctors."

Chinese proverb

MACARONI AND SALMON

2 Slices Stale Wheat Bread
1 Garlic Clove
1 tsp Fish Seasoning
Pepper

2 Tb Butter, melted

2 Cups Cooked Pasta Elbows (1 heaping cup dry)
1 14 3/4 oz can Salmon, drained and cleaned
  (discard any skin or vertebrae)
1 1/2 Cups Milk
2 Tb Parmesan Cheese

▲ Process or blend Bread, Garlic, Fish Seasoning and Pepper
  until bread-crumb consistency is reached
▲ Toss in melted Butter until thoroughly coated
▲ Layer Pasta Elbows and Salmon in a casserole dish
▲ Pour Milk over evenly
▲ Sprinkle Seasoned Bread Crumbs over
▲ Sprinkle with Parmesan
▲ Bake at 350 degrees for 50 minutes

4 Servings

Calories: 434
Protein: 30
Carbs: 38
Fat: 17

Very mild, very delicous. Made canned salmon, which we
don't even like, into one of our all-time favorites. Serve
with green beans.

CHEESY BAKED FISH

2 oz Sharp Cheddar
3 Slices stale Wheat Bread
1 Garlic clove
1/2 tsp Fish Seasoning
3 Tb Vegetable Oil
1 1/2 lbs firm White Fish (Icelandic Cod, or Halibu
for example)

▲ Wash fish and pat dry, cut in wedges a bit larger then fish-
sticks
▲ Process or blend first four ingredients until a bread-crumb
consistency is reached
▲ Dip Fish pieces first in Oil, then in crumb mixture
▲ Place on cookie sheet, sprinkle any leftover crumbs over
fish
▲ Bake at 450 degrees for 10-12 minutes

4 Servings

Calories: 379
Protein: 45
Carbs: 10
Fat: 17

Delicious, and I don't even like fish!

UN-FISH

3 Tb Butter
3 Green Onions, chopped
1/2 Onion, sliced
1/2 lb Mushrooms, sliced (about 2 1/2 cups)
1 Garlic clove, minced
1 Tb Parsley, chopped
1/4 cup dry White Wine
juice from 1/2 Lemon
Fish Seasoning
3 Red Snapper Filets (about a pound)
2 Yams, peeled

▲ Put Yams in water to boil, they take about 45 min, until a fork penetrates easily
▲ Saute Onions, Mushrooms, Garlic and Parsley in Butter a few minutes
▲ Add Wine, Lemon juice and Seasoning, simmer another minute or so
▲ Push Vegies aside and add Snapper, cook until the edges turn white, then flip and cook until fish turns white and flakes apart easily
▲ Serve Fish and sliced Yams topped with mushrooms and broth

2 Large Servings

Calories: 647
Protein: 63
Carbs: 44
Fat: 23

Fish often can not be filling enough for a person seeking high calorie counts, and the complementary yams take care of that.

MOM'S TUNA CASSEROLE

16 oz Egg Noodles
1 12 1/2 oz can Tuna, drained
1 10 3/4 oz cans of Cream of Mushroom Soup
1 Cup Milk (I use whole, you can use nonfat)
2-3 Celery stalks, diced
10 oz frozen Peas
1/4 tsp Thyme
Pepper to taste
2 Tb Wheat Germ
2 Tb Parmesan Cheese

▲ Put on a large pot of water to boil
▲ Warm Soup in saucepan, stir in Milk
▲ Add Celery, Peas, Thyme and Pepper to Soup
▲ Cook, and drain Noodles well
▲ Spread Noodles into a buttered glass oblong pan (9x 13)
▲ Flake Tuna evenly over Noodles
▲ Pour Soup mixture over Noodles and stir to coat
▲ Sprinkle Wheat Germ over the Parmesan
▲ Bake at 350 degrees for 20-30 minutes

7 Servings

Calories: 396
Protein: 24
Carbs: 52
Fat: 10

What can I say? Great Tuna Casserole!

TUNA TORTILLAS

1 12 1/2 oz Can Tuna, drained
2 Tb Sour Cream
1/2 Avocado
1/4 Cup Salsa
3/4 Cup Shredded Cheddar Cheese
3 Whole Wheat Chapatis (like tortillas only thicker)

▲ Mash Tuna and Sour Cream together well
▲ Mash Avocado and Salsa together in separate bowl
▲ Heat Chapatis in warm oven
▲ Divide Tuna, Avocado and Cheese evenly into Chapatis
▲ Roll into burritos, heat until warm

3 Big Servings

Calories: 443
Protein: 40
Carbs: 27
Fat: 21

Diguises Tuna perfectly!

TUNA MELTS

1 12 1/2 oz can Tuna, drained
1 Sweet Pickle, chopped
1/4 Cup Mayo
1 Tomato, sliced
1/2 Avocado, sliced
9 thin slices Monterey Jack cheese
3 slices Wheat Bread, toasted

▲ Mix Tuna, Pickle and Mayo well
▲ Layer toast with Tomato and Avocado
▲ Mound Tuna mixture evenly over Tomato and Avocado
▲ Top with Cheese and broil until golden

Per Slice

Calories: 627
Protein: 48
Carbs: 18
Fat: 42

Why eat out when cooking is this good?

VINCE GIRONDA'S TUNA SALAD

1 12 1/2 oz can Tuna, drained
1/2 Cucumber, peeled and minced
1/2 Onion, minced
2 Stalks Celery, minced
1/4 tsp Garlic Powder
1/4 Cup Mayo

▲ Mix well
▲ Try serving this with sliced tomato, avocado or on a salad

3 Servings

Calories: 300
Protein: 31
Carbs: 5
Fat: 19

People can say whatever they want about Vince, but to me he's a great guy (and a good cook).

"Everything you see I owe to spaghetti."

Sofia Loren

PASTA

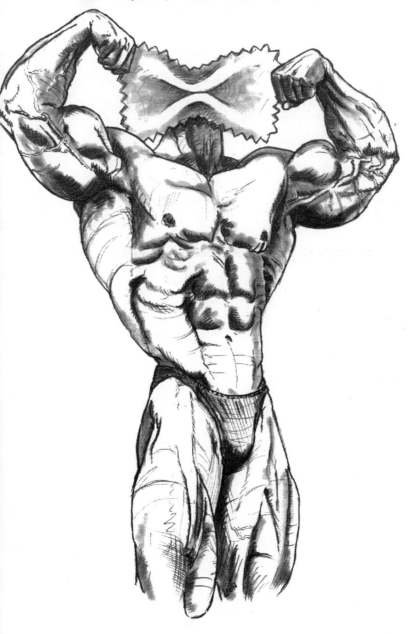

"The trouble with eating Italian food is that five or six days later you're hungry again."

George Miller

LINGUINE WITH FRESH TOMATO

8 oz Linguine (1/2 box)
3-4 Tb Butter
1 large, ripe, chopped Tomato
1/4 tsp Garlic Powder
1/2 tsp Italian Seasoning
1/3 Cup freshly grated Parmesan Cheese

Microwave:
▲ Cook Linguine ahead of time, drain, rinse with cold water. Drain again and keep in a plastic baggie until ready to eat
▲ Microwave pasta in open bag. In separate bowl microwave Butter, Spices and chopped Tomato (include any tomato pulp)
▲ Add Linguine to Butter mixture. Toss, add Cheese, toss again

Stovetop:
▲ Cook Linguine according to package directions, drain
▲ In pan over low heat melt Butter, add Tomato and Spices
▲ Toss all together, add Cheese, toss again

2 Servings

Calories: 682
Protein: 22
Carbs: 87
Fat: 27

With sweet unsalted butter, freshly grated parmesan and a really good tomato this recipe is so good you won't believe it was that easy to make!

CHICKEN LINGUINE

2 Tb Olive Oil
3 Tb Butter
3 Green Onions, chopped
2 Garlic cloves, minced
2 Boneless Chicken Breasts, skinned and cut into
  bite-size pieces
1/4 Cup White Wine
1 Lemon wedge
1/2 tsp dried Basil
few dashes of Cayenne Pepper
1 Zucchini, sliced
1 Tomato, chopped
10 oz Frozen Peas
1/4 Cup Parmesan Cheese
1 1 lb box Linguine

▲ Put water on to boil
▲ Saute Garlic and Green Onions in Butter and Oil
▲ Add Chicken, Basil and White Wine, simmer for about 5 min
▲ Put in Linguine to boil
▲ Add Zucchini and Tomato to Chicken mixture, simmer and
  stir while Linguine cooks (avoid overcooking, the zucchini
  will get too limp and Chicken will get dry). Turn the heat
  down low
▲ Drain Linguine well, toss Chicken mixture, Linguine and
  Cheese in a large bowl

6 Large Servings

Calories: 246
Protein: 30
Carbs: 61
Fat: 15

Good workout food, lots of carbs but still not heavy.

LINGUINE WITH CLAMS

3 Tb Butter
3 Tb Olive Oil
3 Garlic cloves, minced
1 6 1/2 oz can minced Clams, partially drained
1/4 tsp dried Basil
1/4 tsp dried Oregano
1/4 Cup freshly grated Parmesan Cheese
8 oz Linguine

▲ Put a large pot of water to boil
▲ Heat Butter and Oil in skillet
▲ Add Garlic and saute briefly
▲ Add Clams and clam juice, Basil, Oregano and half the Parmesan
▲ Reduce heat and keep warm
▲ Boil pasta according to directions. Drain and toss with Clam sauce
▲ Transfer to warmed plates and top with remaining Parmesan

2 Servings

Calories: 861
Protein: 27
Carbs: 87
Fat: 45

Yes, the fat content is high, but the carbs are also very high, which means the fat will bring with it energy. It's up to you to burn it off in the right proportion.

BROCCOLI FETTUCINE

12 oz box Spinach Fettucine noodles
3 Cups Broccoli, chopped
3 Tb Butter
3 Garlic cloves, crushed
1/2 tsp dried Basil
1 16 oz container lowfat Cottage Cheese
1/4 cup Heavy Cream
1 Lemon wedge
1/3 cup Parmesan Cheese, freshly grated

▲ Put on a large pot of water to boil
▲ Blanch the Broccoli (to blanch the Broccoli put it into the hot water briefly, about 30 seconds. It will turn bright green, but still be very crunchy)
▲ Saute the Garlic in the Butter
▲ Add the Basil, Cottage Cheese, Cream and Lemon Juice
▲ Simmer and stir for a couple of minutes, melting the Cottage Cheese
▲ Lower the heat to just below a simmer and keep warm while Pasta cooks
▲ Toss Fettucine and sauce in a large bowl, transfer to warmed plates and top with Parmesan Cheese

4 Servings

Calories: 615
Protein: 31
Carbs: 72
Fat: 24

This makes a thick and gooey sauce. If you prefer it thinner add a small amount of milk. Very good microwave leftovers.

CHILI PEPPER PASTA

5 Tb Butter
2 Tb Olive Oil
1 Onion, sliced
3 Garlic cloves, minced
2 boneless Chicken Breasts, skinned and cut into
  bite-size pieces
1/2 tsp crushed Red Pepper
2 Bell Peppers, thinly sliced (red, green or both)
28 oz can Chopped Tomatoes
2 Tb Chili Powder
1 1lb box of Linguine
6 Tb Parmesan Cheese, freshly grated

▲ Put on a large pot of water to boil (for Linguine)
▲ Heat Butter and Oil in large skillet
▲ Add Onions and Garlic, saute until Onion is wilted (looks transparent)
▲ Add Chicken and Red Pepper, saute until Chicken is no longer pink
▲ Add Tomatoes, Chili Powder, and Bell Peppers
▲ Stir well, lower heat and simmer, stirring occasionally, for about 20 minutes
▲ Boil Linguine according to package directions, drain
▲ Transfer pasta to warmed plates, top with sauce and sprinkle with Parmesan Cheese

6 Servings

Calories: 515
Protein: 33
Carbs: 71
Fat: 10

You can't go wrong with this one. It's kind of spicy, so to cut back go light on the Red Pepper.

FRESH VEGETABLE PASTA SALAD

1 lb box medium Pasta Shells
1.5 oz pignolias (Pine Nuts)
1/2 Cup grated Parmesan Cheese
1/3 Cup Olive Oil
1/3 Cup Red Wine Vinegar
2 Carrots, shredded
1 Zucchini, shredded
1 Bell Pepper, chopped
1 Red Onion, finely chopped
1 Garlic clove, minced
5 or 6 fresh Basil leaves, chopped (scissors work well)

▲ Cook the pasta according to directions, rinse well in cold water (don't overcook)
▲ Roast the Pine Nuts in a dry cast iron skillet until golden
▲ Toss all the ingredients together in a large bowl

Approximately 10 Servings

Calories: 290
Protein: 9
Carbs: 39
Fat: 5

Improvise! Add your own favorites, this is a good recipe you can build on.

SALMON PASTA

1 Package Pasta Shells
2 Cups Blanched Broccoli (see Broccoli Fettucini
   for blanching directions)
1 Bell Pepper, chopped
1/4 Cup Sweet Pickles, chopped
1 15.5 oz can Pink Salmon, cleaned and crumbled
1/3 cup Mayonnaise
2 Tb Honey
1 Cup cubed Swiss Cheese

▲ Heat water to boiling and blanch Broccoli
▲ Cook Pasta, drain and rinse with cold water (don't overcook)
▲ Mix together Mayo, Honey and Sweet Pickles
▲ Put all ingredients in a large bowl and stir to coat

6 Servings

Calories: 453
Protein: 28
Carbs: 36
Fat: 20

This is my husband's favorite. Perfect hot weather food.

BETTER THAN SPAGHETTI

1 lb Ground Beef
1 Chopped Onion
2 Garlic Cloves, crushed
1 26 oz jar Classico Mushroom and Olive spaghetti
  sauce
1 Tb Italian seasoning
few splashes of Red Wine Vinegar
1 Tb Olive Oil
1 box Rotelle (Ronzoni) or Rotini (Creamette) pasta
  cooked according to package directions
1 Cup grated Mozzarella Cheese

▲ Brown Hamburger, Onion and Garlic, drain
▲ Add Spaghetti Sauce, Seasoning, Oil and Vinegar
▲ Reduce heat, simmer while pasta cooks
▲ Toss Pasta, Sauce and Cheese in a large bowl

6 Large Servings

Calories: 638
Protein: 36
Carbs: 70
Fat: 22

Try this served with fresh garlic bread. (Smother sliced
french bread with butter, crushed garlic, and freshly grated
parmesan. Broil until golden brown)

UDON WITH PEANUT SAUCE

1 12 oz package Udon noodles*
1/2 Cup chunky Peanut Butter
1/2 Cup Soy Sauce
Cayenne Pepper
16 oz package frozen Oriental Vegies

▲ Boil Udon according to package directions
▲ Steam Vegies, drain
▲ In saucepan heat Peanut Butter, Soy Sauce and enough
  Cayenne Pepper to make it spicy (to taste)
▲ Add enough water to thin the sauce to the desired consis-
  tency
▲ Toss Udon, Vegies and Sauce together until evenly coated

4 Servings
*Breakdown not available

This recipe sounds weird but it's really good. Honest.

*You can often find Udon in the Oriental aisle of your supermarket.

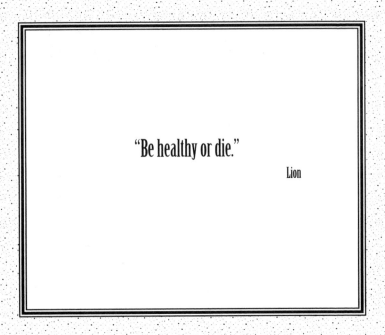

"Be healthy or die."

Lion

POTATOES

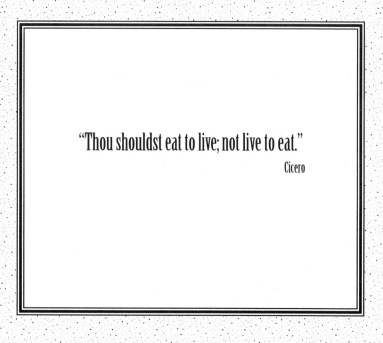

"Thou shouldst eat to live; not live to eat."

Cicero

POTATO MASH

4 large Potatoes, sparsely peeled
1/3 Cup Milk
2 Tb Butter
1/2 Cup Sour Cream
3/4 Cup Cheddar Cheese, shredded
10 oz package frozen Peas, thawed

▲ Boil the Potatoes until done (approx 45 min), when a fork penetrates easily
▲ Drain, add Milk and Butter, mash well
▲ Stir in Sour Cream, Peas and Cheddar

5 servings

Calories: 268
Protein: 10
Carbs: 31
Fat: 14

Feel free to add your favorite vegies, corn, green beans or even lima beans (high in protein). Try the frozen package of mixed vegies for variety.

BAKED POTATO SUPREME

2 Baked Potatoes
1 10 oz package frozen Spinach, warmed and
    thoroughly drained
3/4 Cup grated Cheddar

▲ Beat up potatoes on the counter, slice down the middle
▲ Top With Spinach and Cheese

2 Servings

Calories: 428
Protein: 18
Carbs: 58
Fat: 14

Makes baked potatoes not only edible, but enjoyable.

POTATO SALAD

5 Boiled Potatoes
4 Hard Boiled Eggs
2 Carrots, grated
10 oz frozen Peas, thawed
1/2 Purple Onion, chopped
2 stalks Celery
2 Garlic cloves, minced
1/2 Cup Mayonnaise
1 Tsp Mustard

▲ Boil Potatoes until done, no need to peel.
▲ Cool and chop into small cubes
▲ Mix all ingredients in a large bowl
▲ Chill

7 Large Servings

Calories: 345
Protein: 8
Carbs: 43
Fat: 16

Very filling, hearty enough to constitute a meal.

SUPER SPUDS

4 Large Baked Potatoes
1 Cup Cheddar, shredded
1 Cup Cottage Cheese
1 1/2 Tb Mustard
3 Tb Mayo
3 Hard Boiled Eggs
several dashes of Cayenne Pepper

▲ Bake the Potatoes, scoop out the centers into a bowl
▲ Mix the Potato meat with the other ingredients
▲ Fill the shells with the mixture and
▲ Bake at 350 degrees for 20 minutes

Per Potato

Calories: 524
Protein: 25
Carbs: 55
Fat: 23

Absolutely perfect for microwave snacks.

POTATO AND YAM SOUP

1 Large Yam, peeled
1 Large Potato, peeled
1 Large Onion, chopped
1 Tb Butter
Garlic powder
Vegetable Seasoning
Pepper

▲ Cut Potatoes and Yams in chunks
▲ Saute Onion in Butter
▲ Add Yam and Potato, sprinkle generously with spices
▲ Add just enough water to cover
▲ Cook until vegies are soft, about 40 minutes
▲ Puree with blender, food processor or hand-held blender

Approx 5 Servings

Calories: 100
Protein: 2
Carbs: 18
Fat: 3

This is really good and easy to digest, very soothing and also very filling, even though light in calories. What little fat there is comes from the butter.

HEARTY LENTIL AND POTATO SOU

6 Cups Vegetable Stock
1 Onion, chopped
2 Garlic cloves, minced
2 Tb Olive Oil
3 Carrots, chopped
3 Potatoes, chopped
2 Cups Lentils
1 Tb Parsley, chopped
1/2 Tb Marjoram
1/2 Tb Thyme
1 Bay Leaf
Cayenne Pepper to taste

▲ Saute the Onion and Garlic in Olive Oil until the Onion is wilted
▲ Add Vegetable Stock and remaining ingredients
▲ Simmer about an hour

Approx 6 Servings

Calories: 217
Protein: 9
Carbs: 45
Fat: 5

What do ya know, another recipe with a low fat count!

"A handful of patience is worth more than a bushel of brains."

Dutch proverb

"Health nuts are going to feel stupid some-
day lying in hospitals dying of nothing."

Redd Foxx

POULTRY

"They should stop calling Reagan and Gorbachev the two most powerful men in the world. Between the two of them they couldn't bench press a hundred pounds."

Al Ordover

ITALIAN CHICKEN

3 Chicken Breasts, boneless and skinless
1/2 Cup Italian Salad Dressing
Black Pepper

▲ Marinate the Chicken overnight or while at work
▲ Bake for approx 45 min at 350 degrees

Per Breast

Calories: 327
Protein: 54
Carbs: 2
Fat: 10

Don't let the simplicity of this recipe fool you into thinking it's not that great. This is good enough for guests. I like Bernstein's Italian dressing.

ISLAND CHICKEN

3 Chicken Breasts, skinless and boneless cut into
   bite-size pieces
Marinade:
3 Tomatoes, cut into wedges
4 Green Onions, chopped
1/2 Cup Parsley, chopped
2 Garlic cloves, minced
1/4 tsp Thyme
1/4 Cup White Wine Vinegar
1 Tb Worchestershire sauce
1 Tb Oil

3 Tb Oil
1/4 Cup packed Brown Sugar
2 cups Water
3 Tb Ketchup

Approx 6 Cups Rice, cooked

▲ Marinate Chicken overnight in covered casserole dish
▲ Heat Oil in skillet, add Brown Sugar. Cook until Sugar
   melts and begins to bubble
▲ Add one cup Water, stir and cook until Sugar dissolves
▲ Add remaining Water and Ketchup, stir well
▲ Add Sugar mixture to Chicken in casserole dish, stir well
▲ Bake at 375 degrees for approx 1 hour
▲ Serve over Rice

Approx 8 Servings (3/4 Cup Rice each serving)

Calories:	386
Protein:	25
Carbs:	48
Fat:	10

Gets better each day you eat it!

BAKED CHICKEN

2 Chicken Breasts, boned, skinned, and cut in half
2/3 Cup Italian Bread Crumbs (I like Progresso)
1 Egg, beaten

▲ Wash and pat dry Chicken
▲ Dip in Egg
▲ Dip in Bread Crumbs, covering well
▲ Bake on a buttered cookie sheet (actually, I use my glass
  oblong pan) at 350 degrees for 20 minutes, flip, then bake
  20 minutes more

2 Servings

Calories: 509
Protein: 64
Carbs: 36
Fat: 11

So good you won't even miss Colonel Sanders.

TOMATO CHICKEN WITH BROWN RICE

2 Chicken Breasts, skinless and boneless, chopped
   into bite-size pieces
1 14 oz can Italian style Stewed Tomatoes
1 Bell Pepper, chopped
1 Onion, chopped
1/2 Cup Red Wine
1 tsp dried Basil
1 tsp dried Oregano
2 Garlic cloves, crushed
Pepper, a few dashes
2 Tb Parmesan Cheese, grated

▲ Mix all ingredients except the Cheese in a casserole dish
▲ Sprinkle the Cheese on top
▲ Bake 350 degrees for 45 minutes
▲ Serve over cooked brown rice

4 Servings

Calories: 471
Protein: 34
Carbs: 58
Fat: 6

Easy, easy to make and just as easy to eat. Great left-overs.

CHICKEN ENCHILADAS

2 Chicken Breasts
28 oz can Enchilada Sauce
1 Onion, chopped
1 Cup shredded Jack Cheese
1 6 oz can sliced Black Olives
1 4 oz can Diced Green Chilis
9 Corn Tortillas

▲ Boil Breasts (about 40 min).
▲ Cool, then shred or chop meat, removing skin and bones
▲ Pour a generous amount of sauce in a skillet and heat
▲ Dip Tortillas in sauce on both sides, don't leave in the sauce too long or they'll be too soggy to roll. Use tongs.
▲ Place a generous amount of Chicken, some Onions and Chilis in Tortilla
▲ Roll up and place seam side down in an oblong glass pan
▲ Pour any remaining Enchilada Sauce, Chicken, and Chilis over the top
▲ Top with Black Olives and Jack Cheese
▲ Bake at 350 degrees for 30 minutes

5 Servings. Breakdown doesn't include Enchilada Sauce as I could not find it anywhere

Calories: 319
Protein: 26
Carbs: 24
Fat: 12

Serve with refried beans and garnish with sour cream. Yummmm.

CHICKEN AND BISCUITS

1 Whole Chicken Breast
1 Tb Butter
2 Celery Stalks, diced
3 Carrots, diced
1/4 tsp Garlic Powder
1/4 tsp Thyme
1 10 3/4 oz can Cream of Chicken Soup
1 Cup Chicken Broth
10-serving container Pillsbury Biscuits (or home-made, if you are industrious)
Pepper (optional)

▲ Boil Chicken until done, about 40 min, remove to cool. Save broth
▲ Saute Celery and Carrot in Butter about 4 minutes, add Garlic and Thyme (and Pepper if desired) and stir well
▲ Remove grease from broth (skim off with a spoon) and add 1 Cup to Vegie/Spice mix
▲ Stir in Soup well
▲ Remove Chicken meat from bone (discard skin), chop and add to Soup mixture
▲ Pour into a casserole dish, top with uncooked biscuits
▲ Bake at 400 degrees for 15 minutes

4 Servings

Calories: 426
Protein: 21
Carbs: 42
Fat: 19

This ranks in the top ten best meals I've come up with!

TURKEY MEATLOAF

2 lbs Ground Turkey
2 Garlic cloves
2 Eggs
1/4 Cup Parsley
2 Tb Parmesan Cheese
1 Tb Capers
1/4 tsp White Pepper
2 slices of stale Wheat Bread
Paprika

With food processor:
▲ Make Bread Crumbs out of bread, fairly fine, remove
▲ Process Garlic, Eggs, Parsley, Capers and Pepper until well blended
▲ Mix all ingredients together (sorry to say hands work best)

Manually:
▲ Mince Garlic, chop Parsley, Capers and Wheat Bread
▲ Mix all ingredients (same technique as above)

▲ Bake at 350 degrees for 1 1/2 Hours

4 Servings

Calories: 414
Protein: 51
Carbs: 11
Fat: 20

Great leftovers microwaved with a slice of mild white cheese on top.

TURKEY MEATBALL SANDWICHES

1 lb Ground Turkey
1 Egg
1/4 Cup Bread Crumbs
1/2 Onion, chopped
1 tsp Italian Seasoning
2 Tb Vegetable Oil
15 1/2 oz jar of your favorite Spaghetti Sauce
1 Cup Mozzarella, shredded
1 small loaf French Bread

▲ Mix Turkey, Egg, Crumbs, Onion and Seasonings together
▲ Make into medium size meatballs (or oblong patties)
▲ Cook in Oil until browned and done (check the middle for pinkness if in doubt) Add any crumbles to the sauce
▲ Cut the French Bread down the middle lengthwise, pull out some of the white bread to make a shell if desired
▲ Put a little Sauce in the shell, top with some Cheese and warm in oven slightly
▲ Top bread with Turkey, Sauce and more Cheese

4 Servings

Calories: 531
Protein: 38
Carbs: 42
Fat: 25

This recipe develops its character, overnight so the next day leftovers are even better then you may remember it from the night before.

SOUTHWESTERN STYLE STUFFED BELLS

3 Red Bell Peppers
1 15 oz Can Chili (Health Valley Spicy Vegetarian
   Chili is great)
1 lb Ground Turkey
1 tsp Chili Powder
Fresh Corn cut from one corn on the cob (approx
   3/4 cup)
Cayenne Pepper to taste
1 Cup Jack Cheese, shredded

▲ Cut Bells in half lengthwise and clean out seeds and stems
▲ Brown Turkey, drain.
▲ Add Chili, Corn and Spices to Turkey and stir well. Add
   Cayenne to taste.
▲ Stuff Bell halves with Chili mixture.
▲ Place in a pan, stuffing up, and top with Cheese.
▲ Bake at 325 degrees for about 30 minutes.

Per Bell Half

Calories: 275
Protein: 25
Carbs: 19
Fat: 12

With a good Chili and fresh corn on the cob these are
superb!

"The secret to staying young is to live honestly,
eat slowly, and lie about your age."

Lucille Ball

SNACKS

"It is not the horse that draws the cart, it's the oats."

Russian proverb

BIGGER BODY BARS

1 Cup Apple Juice Concentrate (the frozen stuff)
1/2 Cup Butter, softened
1 tsp Vanilla
3 Eggs
2 cups Whole Wheat Flour
1 Cup Raw Wheat Germ
1/2 tsp Baking Powder
1/2 tsp Baking Soda
1 cup Sunflower Seeds
1 cup Pecans, chopped
1 cup Raisins
1 cup Dates, chopped

▲ Blend Juice, Butter, Vanilla and Eggs
▲ Sift together the Flour, Wheat Germ, Baking Powder and Soda
▲ Add to first mixture and stir well
▲ Add remaining ingredients and mix well
▲ Press into a buttered 9x13 glass oblong pan
▲ Bake at 350 degrees about 30 minutes, until top is golden brown
▲ Refrigerate to keep fresh

About 12 Bars

Calories: 437
Protein: 11
Carbs: 53
Fat: 24

A pain in the you-know-what to make, but they last for days and are the best snacks—mini-meals.

ENERGY BARS

1 Cup Peanut Butter
1 Cup Honey
1 Cup Protein Powder
3 Cups Raw Wheat Germ

▲ Mix it all together and press into a glass oblong pan or a
Tupperware dish with a lid, refrigerate and enjoy

For 15 squares

Calories: 307
Protein: 15
Carbs: 42
Fat: 78

Any Protein Powder is fine, but I like chocolate Metabolol.

DATE BREAD

1 1/2 Cups of boiling Water
2 Cups Dates, chopped
4 Cups Whole Wheat Flour
2 Tsp Baking Soda
2 Eggs
3 Tb Butter, melted
1 Cup Honey
1 Tb Vanilla
1 Cup Pecans, chopped

▲ Pour boiling Water over Dates and let them sit for 30 min
▲ Stir together Flour and Baking Soda
▲ Stir together Eggs, Butter, Honey and Vanilla
▲ Add Date mixture, stir well
▲ Add Pecans, stir well
▲ Bake in a buttered 9x13 glass oblong pan at
325 degrees for about 45 minutes

15 Pieces

Calories: 304
Protein: 5
Carbs: 58
Fat: 7

Refrigerate leftovers and cut the pieces as you serve them to prevent them from drying out.

BRAN BANANA BREAD

1 Cup Whole Wheat Flour
1 Cup Unbleached White Flour
1 tsp Baking Soda
1/2 tsp Salt

1/2 Cup soft Butter
3/4 Cup Honey
2 Eggs

2 large Bananas, mashed
1 1/2 Cups Bran (can use Bran cereal)

3/4 Cup Pecans, chopped
3/4 Cup Raisins

▲ Sift first 4 ingredients together into a large bowl
▲ Stir Honey and Butter together, add Eggs, stir well
▲ Mix Bananas and Bran together well
▲ Add Honey mix and Banana mix to Flour mix and stir well
▲ Add Pecans and Raisins
▲ Bake in a buttered and floured glass loaf pan at
  350 degrees for 50-60 minutes

Per slice for 10 slices

Calories: 433
Protein: 10
Carbs: 77
Fat: 15

This is great for breakfast with a glass of milk. To make it into more of a dessert-type bread add chocolate chips.

RICE SALAD

1 cup uncooked Rice
3 Hard-boiled Eggs
3 Celery stalks
1 Green or Red Bell Pepper
1 Bunch Green Onions
1 3 oz jar of Spanish Olives
1 Small can sliced Black Olives
1 Tb Parsley
1/2 Cup Mayonnaise

▲ Cook Rice until just tender
▲ Chop the Eggs, Celery, Bell Pepper, Green Onions, Olives and Parsley
▲ Mix everything together in a large bowl and refrigerate until well chilled

5 Large Servings

Calories: 371
Protein: 8
Carbs: 29
Fat: 26

You would never guess that rice can taste this good.

BEET AND CARROT CASSEROLE

3 large Beets
1/2 lb Carrots
5 Tb Butter
1 1/2 Bunches Green Onions, chopped (greens included)
3 Garlic cloves, minced
1/2 lb Cheddar Cheese, grated

▲ Steam Beets whole (scrub them clean first, and cut off the ends) for about 15 minutes
▲ Add Carrots (scrubbed, with ends removed) and steam both just until a fork will penetrate
▲ Saute Onions and Garlic in Butter until Onions become very limp
▲ Grate the Carrots and Beets into an oblong glass pan, keeping the two separate until mixing time
▲ Add Onion and Butter mixture
▲ Toss all together to coat, and top with Cheese
▲ Broil until Cheese is golden brown

Approx 6 Servings

Calories: 302
Protein: 12
Carbs: 14
Fat: 23

This is somewhat tedious to make, but you will not regret the effort. Try serving it with black beans and hearty wheat bread.

BEANO BURRITOS

1 Tb Butter
1 Onion, chopped
1 Can Vegetarian Refried Beans
1/2 Cup Rice
1/4 Cup Salsa
1 Tomato, chopped
1 Cup Cheddar Cheese, grated
6 Flour Tortillas

▲ Saute Onion in Butter until limp, about 3 minutes
▲ Add Beans, Rice, Salsa and Tomato. Heat and stir
▲ Heat Tortillas one at a time in a large skillet
▲ Put a couple of spoonfuls of the Beans down the middle, top with Cheese and roll up. Keep in warm oven until they are all ready.

Per Burrito

Calories: 245
Protein: 10
Carbs: 34
Fat: 9

These are so good it's easy to eat too much and regret it!

POWER PANCAKES

Regular Pancake mix for 4 servings
1/4 Cup Sunflower Seeds
1/4 Cup Raisins
1/3 Cup Oats
1/2 Cup Wheat Germ

Topping:
2 Bananas, mashed
1/4 cup Honey
1 Tb Jam (I like blueberry)

▲ Prepare mix according to directions
▲ Add the rest and mix well
▲ Grill
▲ Mash topping ingredients together

2 Hearty Servings

Calories: 747
Protein: 21
Carbs: 137
Fat: 18

Guaranteed, no hunger pains until lunchtime.

"The greatest pleasure in life is doing
what people say you cannot do ."
Walter Bagehot

"Even if you're on the right track, you'll get run over if you just sit there"

Will Rogers

PROTEIN
DRINKS

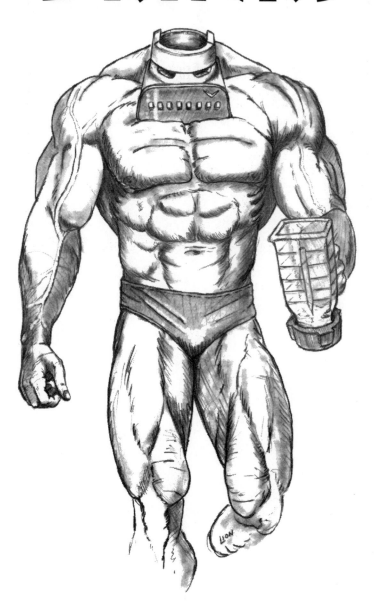

"He who makes no mistakes never makes anything."

English proverb

THE BASIC BLASTER

2 Cups Milk
2 Eggs
2 Tb Nonfat Powdered Milk
2 Tb Honey
2 Tb Yeast
2 Frozen Bananas

2 Hearty Servings

Per Serving
Calories: 460
Protein: 25
Carbs: 65
Fat: 14

Too good to be a Protein Drink.

THE NO-FRILLS DRINK

8 oz Half n Half
8 oz Yogurt
3 Eggs
1/2 Cup Powdered Milk
1/2 Cup Protein Powder (we used NSP Milk & Egg)

2 Servings

Per Serving
Calories: 470
Protein: 38
Carbs: 23
Fat: 24

PEANUT BUTTER BOMBER

1 1/2 Cups Milk
2 Tb Peanut Butter
1 Tb Yeast
1/2 Cup Powdered Milk
1/2 Cup Protein Powder
2 Tb Honey
1 Frozen Banana

2 Servings

Per Serving
Calories: 471
Protein: 35
Carbs: 55
Fat: 15

Why have a milkshake when a Pro-Drink can taste this good

BLUEBERRY SPECIAL

2 Cups Milk
1 Banana
1 Cup Frozen Blueberries
1/2 Cup Milk Powder
2 Tb Lecithin Granules
1 Tb Honey

2 Servings

Per Serving
Calories: 390
Protein: 16
Carbs: 54
Fat: 15

...and you could always add ice cream....

HUMMMDINGER

1 1/2 Cups Fresh-Squeezed Orange Juice
1/2 cup water
1 Frozen Banana
1 cup Ice Cream

2 Servings

Per Serving
Calories: 270
Protein: 4
Carbs: 49
Fat: 8

An absolutely incredibly delicious pre-workout drink.

STRAWBERRY PRO

2 Cups Milk
1 Banana
1 Cup Frozen Strawberries
1/2 cup Protein Powder
1 Tb Yeast

2 Servings

Per Serving
Calories: 307
Protein: 26
Carbs: 35
Fat: 9

This isn't sweet at all, so if you have a sweet tooth add
some honey or ice cream if you can afford the calories.

RICHEY RICH

1 Cup Milk
1 Cup Cream
2 Eggs
1 Cup Powdered Milk
1 Frozen Banana

3 Servings

Per Serving
Calorie: 500
Protein: 17
Carbs: 28
Fat: 36

As rich as Arnold! Watch that waistline with this baby.

THE SUPER SQUATS DRINK
(COURTESY RANDALL STROSSEN)

4 cups Whole Milk
2 Cups of Powdered Milk
1/4 Cup Nutritional Yeast
1 Banana
2 Tb Lecithin
1 Tb Wheat Germ Oil
1 large scoop vanilla Ice Cream

Whole Thing:

Calories: 1890
Protein: 121
Carbs: 209
Fat: 76

Yep, that's a lot of Fat, but have you ever tried Randall's
Super Squats routine? That fat will not have time to settle!

"Three out of four doctors recommend another doctor"

Graffito

GAINER'S GOURMET

Lion Attitude
P.O.Box 2055
Venice, CA 90294

NAME _____

STREET _____

CITY _____

STATE _____ ZIP _____

Please send _____ copies of Gainer's Gourmet at $12.95
per copy and $3.50 to cover postage and handling ($5 outside
the US please). CA residents add $1.07 sales tax. Make check
or money order payable to: Lion Attitude. Credit card orders call
1-800-447-0008.

— ⋅ — ⋅ — ⋅ — ⋅ — ⋅ — ⋅ — ⋅ — ⋅ — ⋅ — ⋅ — ⋅ — ⋅ ✂

GAINER'S GOURMET

Lion Attitude
P.O.Box 2055
Venice, CA 90294

NAME _____

STREET _____

CITY _____

STATE _____ ZIP _____

Please send _____ copies of Gainer's Gourmet at $12.95
per copy and $3.50 to cover postage and handling ($5 outside
the US please). CA residents add $1.07 sales tax. Make check
or money order payable to: Lion Attitude. Credit card orders call
1-800-447-0008.

#1

#2

"Who's That Girl?"

A must for your home, office, and gym. If you already have *#One* you'll really want *#Two*, if not order both now!

#1 Full color 20" x 28" polychrome print.
#2 Hand-tinted 16" x 20" print on extremely high-grade paper stock.

ONLY $10.95 ea.
or $16.95 for both!! *(You save $4.95*)

+ $2.75 postage & handling for one or $3.50 for both.

CA residents please add $.90 sales tax.
Foreign orders add $5.00 S&H. U.S. currency only.

Don't forget to vote

ORDER FROM: **LION ATTITUDE**
P.O. Box 2055, Venice, CA 90294